How-To-Crochet Snowflakes

Easy crochet snowflakes using basic crochet stitches

Easy Crochet Patterns

Volume 1

Vicki Becker

Copyright © 2016 Vicki Becker. All rights reserved worldwide

Copyright © 2016 Vicki Becker. All rights reserved worldwide.

No part of this publication may be replicated, redistributed, or given away in any form or by any means, including scanning, photocopying, or otherwise without the prior written consent of the copyright holder.

You have permission to sell items you personally make from the patterns but not for commercial or mass production purposes. You do not, however, have permission to use my photographs to sell your items.

All patterns are sold in good faith. Every effort has been made to ensure that all instructions are accurate and complete.

ISBN-13: 978-1539689706

ISBN-10: 1539689700

First Printing, 2016
Printed in the United States of America

Contents

Gold and White Lace Snowflake..Page 13

Gold and White Picot Star Snowflake..Page 15

Silver Lace Snowflake..Page 17

Little Gold and White Snowflake..Page 19

Silver Splendor Snowflake..Page 21

Gold and White Ruffled Snowflake..Page 23

Silver and White Picot Star Snowflake......................................Page 25

Silver Sparkle Snowflake..Page 27

Crochet Snowflakes!

This crochet pattern book contains instructions for 8 original snowflake designs. You can crochet these quick and easy thread ornaments for your Christmas tree or to use as package toppers.

General Instructions

Basic Crochet Stitches

Sl st - slip stitch: With loop on hook, insert hook in st or space indicated and draw yarn through both the st and loop on hook.

Sc - Single Crochet: With loop on hook, insert hook in st or space indicated, draw yarn through 2 loops on hook, yo hook and pull through both loops on hook.

Hdc - Half Double Crochet: With loop on hook, yo hook and insert in st or space indicated, draw yarn through 3 loops on hook, yo and pull through all 3 loops on hook.

Dc - Double Crochet: With loop on hook, yo hook and insert in st or space indicated, draw yarn through 3 loops on hook, yo and pull through 2 loops, yo and pull through 2 remaining loops.

Tr - Treble Crochet: With loop on hook, yo hook **twice** and insert in st indicated, draw yarn through 4 loops on hook, * yo and pull through 2 loops; repeat from * until only 1 loop remains on hook.

Dtr - Double Treble Crochet: With loop on hook, yo hook **3 times** and insert in st or space indicated, draw yarn through 5 loops on hook * yo and pull through 2 loops; repeat from * until only 1 loop remains on hook.

Changing Colors

To change color in singe or double crochet always work the last two loops on the hook off with the new color.

For single crochet, pull up a loop in the current color you are sing, draw the new color through the last two loops on the hook to complete the single crochet stitch.

For double crochet, yarn over, pull up a loop in the current color you are using, draw through two loops, drawthe new color through the last two loops on the hook to complete the double crochet stitch.

Gauge

Gauge is determined by the tightness or looseness of your work and will affect the finished size of your project. Make a small section of the pattern before starting your project to check the gauge.

Understanding Symbols

An asterisk (*), double asterisk (**), or dagger (†) indicates that the instructions immediately following are to be repeated the given number of times in addition to the original.

Brackets [ ] indicate that all instructions within brackets are to be worked the number of times given after the bracket.

Parenthesis is used to set off a group of instructions worked a number of times or in a particular stitch. For example, "(3 dc, ch 1, 3 dc) in each corner" or "(3 dc, ch 3) 3 times".

Motif Centers

After making the center ring I always crochet over the tail end of the yarn. I can then pull the end of the yarn to make a nice tight center.

Standard Yarn Weight System

Most yarn and thread now come with a weight number on the wrapper. I provide the weight number of the yarn or thread used for each pattern. This makes it much easier to make substitutions. Skill level and yarn weight graphics are provided by http://www.yarnstandards.com

Blocking

To block acrylic yarn projects you need to use steam. The steam dampens the project and heats it. The synthetic fibres in the yarn get fixed when they are heated and then cool down again. To steam block a crochet project made with acrylic yarn first pin it out to the correct size on a blocking board with rust proof pins. Set your iron to the hottest setting with steam. Holding the iron about an inch away from the crochet move the iron slowly over the crochet Don't hold the iron too close or touch the crochet with the iron as this will melt the yarn and ruin your work. Remove your project from the board after it is completely dry.

Blocking items made with acrylic yarns is not absolutly nessesary but it will give your crochet a professional finished look.

Skill Levels

Beginner
A beginner project is for first-time crocheters using basic stitches. Beginner projects have minimal shaping.

Beginner / Débutant / Novicecia

Easy
Easy projects use yarn with basic stitches, repetitive stitch patterns, simple color changes, with simple shaping and finishing.

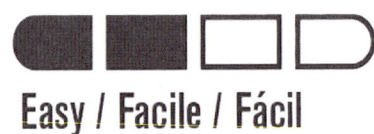
Easy / Facile / Fácil

Intermediate
Intermediate projects use a variety of techniques, such as basic lace patterns or color patterns. This level has mid-level shaping and finishing.

Intermediate / Intermédiaire / Intermedio

Experienced
Projects for experienced crocheters have intricate stitch patterns, techniques and dimension, such as non-repeating patterns, multi-color techniques, fine threads, small hooks, detailed shaping and refined finishing.

Experienced / Experimenté / Experiencia

Abbreviations

beg	begin, beginning	MC	main color
bet	between	mm	millimeter (s)
BL	back loop (s)	oz	ounce
Bpdc	back post double crochet	p	picot
CA	color A	PM	place marker
CB	color B	pat (s)	patterns (s)
CC	contrasting color	rem	remaining
ch	chain stitch	rep (s)	repeat (s)
CL	cluster	RS	right side
dc	double crochet	sc	single crochet
dec	decrease	sc2tog	single crochet 2 together
dtr	double treble crochet	sk	skip
FL	front loop (s)	sl st	slip stitch
foll	follow, follows, following	sp (s)	space (s)
Fpdc	front post double crochet	st (s)	stitch (es)
hdc	half double crochet	tog	together
inc	increase	tr	treble crochet
lp (s)	loop (s)	WS	wrong side
		yo	yarn over

British vs American Crochet Terms

UK-British English		US-American English	
dc	double crochet	sc	single crochet
htr	half treble crochet	hdc	half double crochet
tr	treble	dc	double crochet
dtr	double treble	tr	treble
trtr	triple treble	dtr	double treble
	Miss		skip
	tension		gauge
yoh	yarn over hook	yo	yarn over

All pattern instructions use US-American English terms

Plastic Ring Tutorial

Instructions

The snowflakes in this book require you to start by crocheting over a plastic ring. This tutorial is for crocheting over a plastic ring with single crochet. You can crochet over the ring with single crochet, double crochet, triple crochet, or a combination of stitches. If you prefer not to use a plastic ring just start your snowflake by either crocheting a ring or making a magic circle.

Attach the thread to the hook with a slip knot. Then we will make a sl st to attach the thread to the plastic ring.

Join to the plastic ring by first inserting your hook through the center of the ring. The thread lies over the top of the ring. Catch the thread with your hook and draw under the ring and through the loop on your hook to make a sl st. Chain 1 for single crochet or the number of chains indicated in the pattern.

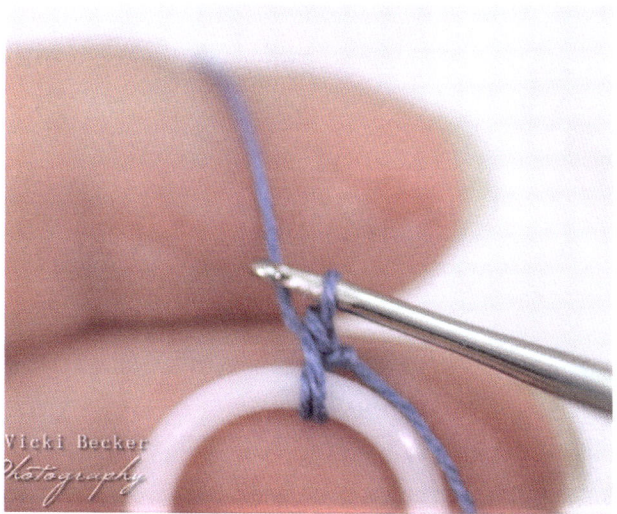

To sc over the ring first insert your hook through the center of the ring, catch the thread with your hook and draw under the ring. Yarn over and draw through the two loops on your hook.

To dc or tr over the ring wrap the thread one or two times around your hook before inserting through the ring.

Sc around the ring crocheting the number of stitches designated in the pattern you are using. Join to the beginning with a slip stitch and continue on with your pattern.

Blocking Snowflakes

Washing and blocking your snowflakes will make a huge difference in how they come out looking in the end. After I make up a bunch of them I soak them over night in a small container that has a lid and a little laundry detergent. Give the container a shake every now and then to agitate. Rinse your snowflakes and lay flat on towels until completely dry.

SNOWFLAKE BLOCKING PATTERN

Blocking snowflakes is much easier with a paper pattern so you can pin the snowflakes out evenly. Copy the paper pattern making several copies to block your snowflakes.

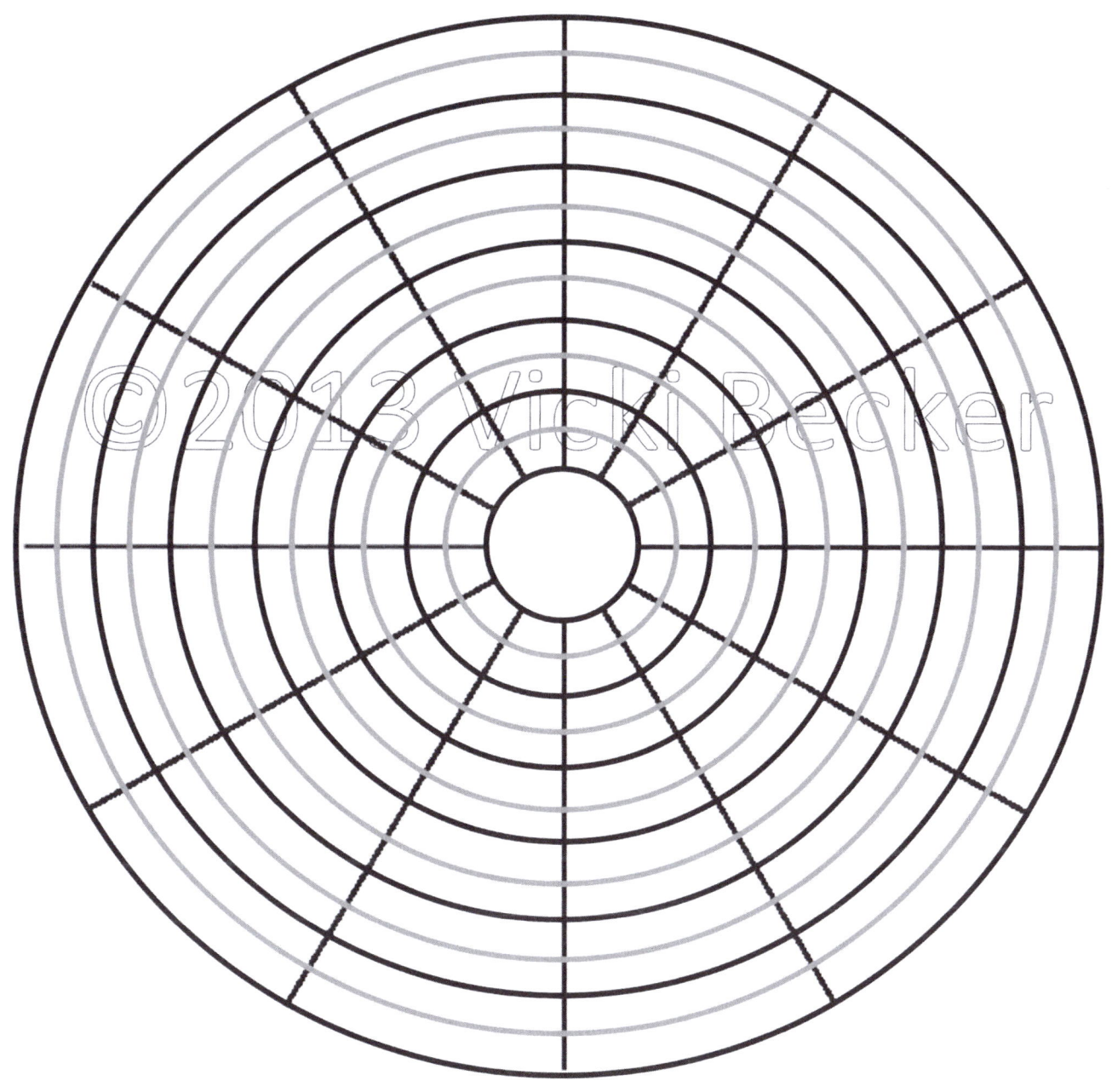

BLOCKING BOARD

The best board for blocking is a foam core "presentation board". You can also use cardboard or Styrofoam but I prefer the presentation board.

PINS

My favorite pins to use are T-pins. T-pins are much heavier than sewing pins so they don't bend and they have a crossbar at the top so they're easy to pull out even if your glue solution sticks the snowflake to them.

Most pins available are nickel plated. Be aware that the plating can wear off and the water in the glue solution can make the pins rust which can stain your snowflakes. Before reusing any pins check them for rust.

Sewing pins are not as good as T-pins. Sewing pins bend easily and are harder to pull out if your stiffener glues them to your snowflakes. The sewing pins with big round heads are better choice but their heads can pull off when removing them from the dried snowflakes. If you have to use sewing pins separate out some to use only for snowflakes. The glue solution gums them up permanently and you can no longer use them for fabric.

BLOCKING

To stiffen and block your snowflakes print out the paper pattern and trim to size. Arrange the paper patterns on the presentation board. Next completely cover your blocking board with wax paper or clear contact paper to prevent the snowflakes from sticking to your board.

Saturate the snowflakes in a solution of 1 part water to 1 part white glue. Squeeze out the excess solution and blot with paper towels. Pin the snowflakes to the blocking board using the paper pattern as a guide. Let your snowflakes dry completely before removing them from the board.

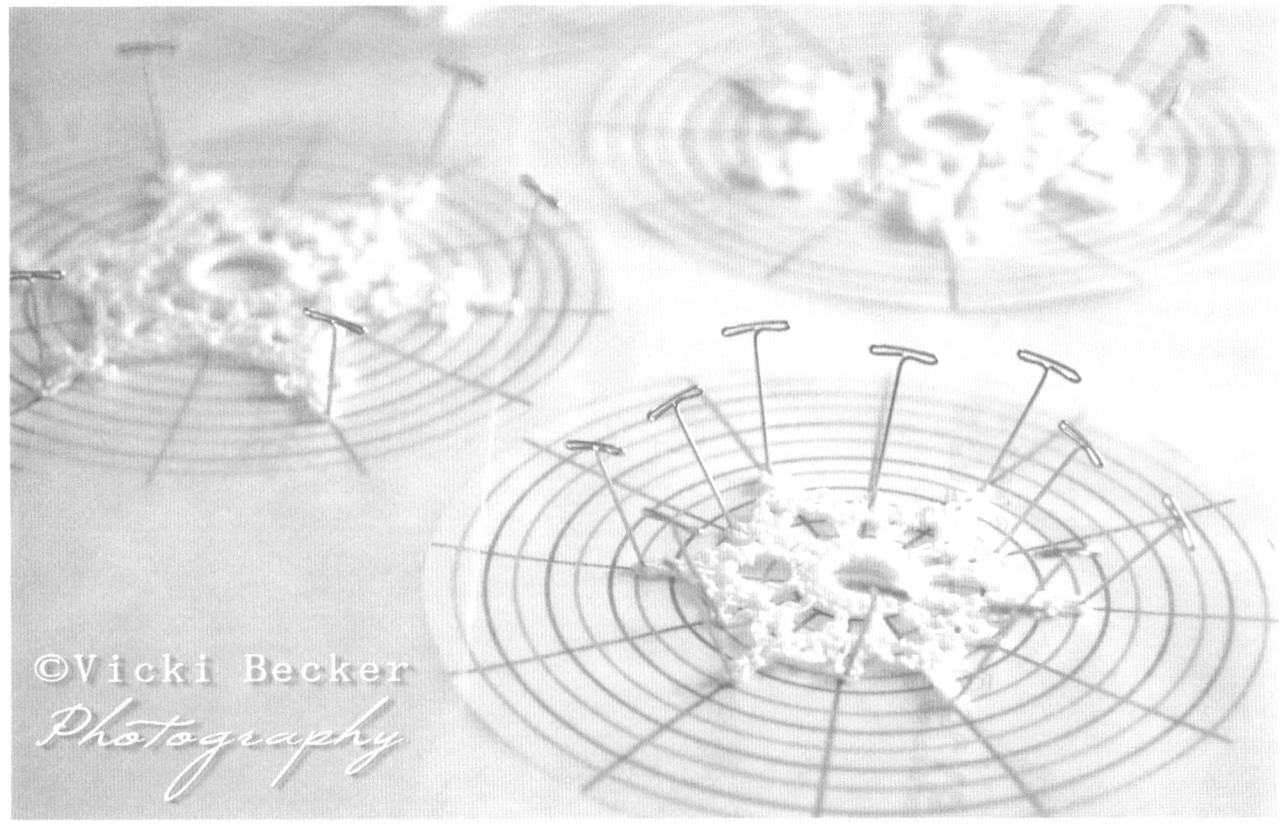

Gold and White Lace Snowflake

Easy / Facile / Fácil

FINISHED MEASUREMENTS
Snowflake is approximately 6 inches after finishing.

MATERIALS
- Coats & Clark Aunt Lydia's Size 10 Metallic Thread

    14 yd White/Pearl

    6 yd Gold/Gold

    5/8" plastic ring
- Hook - 2.00 mm
- Tapestry needle

PATTERN NOTES
See book sections for crocheting over plastic rings and blocking snowflakes if necessary.

SPECIAL STITCHES
Picot: Ch 3, sc in 3rd ch from hook.

INSTRUCTIONS
Rnd 1: Join White/Pearl thread with sl st over plastic ring. Ch 3, work 17 dc over ring. Join with a sl st to top of beg ch-3. 18 dc.

Rnd 2: Ch 1, sc in same st, ch 5, sk next 3 sts, (sc in next st, ch 5, sk next 3 sts) around, join with a sl st in first sc. 6 sc.

Rnd 3: Sl st in first ch sp, (ch 4, 2 tr, ch 3, 3 tr, ch 3, 3 tr, ch 3) in same sp, (3 tr, ch 3) 3 times in each ch sp around. Join with a sl st in top of beg ch-4.

Rnd 4: Sl st in next 2 tr and in first ch sp. (Ch 4, tr, picot, tr) in first ch sp, *ch 3, (2 tr, picot, tr) in next ch sp, ch 5, (sc, picot) in next ch sp, ch 5, (2 tr, picot, tr) in next ch sp, repeat from * around. Join with a sl st in top of beg ch-4. Fasten off.

Rnd 5: With Gold/Gold thread sl st in any ch-3 sp. (Ch 4, 2 tr, picot, 2 tr) in ch-3 sp, *ch 7, sc in next ch-5 sp, ch 7, sl st in 5th ch from hook, ch 2, sc in next ch-5 sp, ch 7, (3 tr, picot, 2 tr) in next ch-3 sp, rep from * around. Join with a sl st to top of beg ch-4. Fasten off.

FINISHING
Weave in ends. Follow directions for stiffening and blocking snowflakes.

Gold and White Picot Star Snowflake

Easy / Facile / Fácil

FINISHED SIZE
Snowflake is approximately 5½" after finishing.

MATERIALS
- Coats & Clark Aunt Lydia's Size 10 Metallic Thread

    10 yd White/Pearl

    6 yd Gold/Gold

- 5/8" plastic ring
- Hook - 2.00 mm
- Tapestry needle

PATTERN NOTES
See book sections for crocheting over plastic rings and blocking snowflakes if necessary.

SPECIAL STITCHES
Beginning Shell: Ch 3, (2 dc, ch 2, 3 dc) in same sp.

Shell: (3 dc, ch 2, 3 dc) in sp indicated.

Triple picot (tr picot): Ch 8, sl st in 8th ch from hook, ch 10, sl st in 10th ch from hook, ch 8, sl st in 8th ch from hook.

Ch-4 picot (ch-4 p): Ch 4, sl st in 4th ch from hook.

INSTRUCTIONS
Rnd 1: Join White/Pearl thread with sl st over plastic ring. Ch 1, work 24 sc over ring. Join with a sl st to first sc. 24 sc.

Rnd 2: Beginning shell in same st as joining, skip next 3 sc, *shell in next sc, skip next 3 sc, rep from * 4 times. Join with a sl st to top of beg ch-3. 6 shells.

Rnd 3: Sl st in 2 dc, (sl st, ch 1, 2 sc) all in first ch-2 sp, ch 8, *(2 sc in next ch-2 sp), ch 8, rep from * 4 times. Join with a sl st to first sc. 6 ch-8 loops.

Rnd 4: Sl st in next sc, (sl st, ch 2, 5 dc, tr, 5 dc, hdc) all in first ch-8 sp, *(hdc, 5 dc, tr, 5 dc, hdc) all in next ch-8 sp, rep from * 4 times. Join to the top of beg ch-2. Fasten off.

Rnd 5: Join Gold/Gold with a sl st in first hdc of any group, ch 1, *sc in next 5 dc, tr picot in next tr, sc in next 5 dc, sl st in next hdc, ch-4 p, ** sl st in next hdc, rep from * around, ending at **. Join with a sl st to first sc. Fasten off.

FINISHING
Weave in ends. Follow directions for stiffening and blocking snowflakes.

Silver Lace Snowflake

Easy / Facile / Fácil

FINISHED MEASUREMENTS
Snowflake is approximately 6½" after finishing.

MATERIALS
- Coats & Clark Aunt Lydia's Size 10 Metallic Thread

    5 yd White/Pearl

    8 yd Silver/Silver

- ½" plastic ring
- Hook - 2.00 mm
- Tapestry needle

PATTERN NOTES
See book sections for crocheting over plastic rings and blocking snowflakes if necessary.

SPECIAL STITCHES
Picot: Ch 3, sc in 3rd ch from hook.

INSTRUCTIONS
Rnd 1: Join White/Silver thread with sl st over plastic ring. Ch 4 (counts as first dc plus ch 1). Work (dc, ch 1) 15 more times over ring. Join with a sl st to 3rd ch of beg ch-4. 16 ch-1 sps.

Rnd 2: Sl st in next ch-1 sp, ch 1, sc in same sp, ch 8, sk next ch-1 sp, * sc in next ch-1 sp, ch 8, skip next ch-1 sp; rep from * around. Join with a sl st to first sc. 8 sc and 8 ch-8 sps.

Rnd 3: Sl st in next 3 chs, ch 1, sc in same sp, ch 10, * sc in next ch-8 sp, ch 10; rep from * around. Join with a sl st to first sc. 8 sc and 8 ch-10 lps.

Rnd 4: With Silver/Silver thread sl st in any ch-10 sp. Ch 1, in same lp and in each lp around work [(sc, picot, sc) twice, ch 4, tr, (ch 6, sl st in 5th ch from hook) 5 times, ch 1, tr, ch 4, sc, (picot, sc) twice]. Join with a sl st to beg sc. Fasten off.

FINISHING
Weave in ends. Follow directions for stiffening and blocking snowflakes.

Little Gold and White Snowflake

Easy / Facile / Fácil

FINISHED MEASUREMENTS
Snowflake is approximately 4½" after finishing.

MATERIALS
- Coats & Clark Aunt Lydia's Size 10 Metallic Thread

    10 yd White/Pearl

    8 yd Gold/Gold

- ½" plastic ring
- Hook - 2.00 mm
- Tapestry needle

PATTERN NOTES
See book sections for crocheting over plastic rings and blocking snowflakes if necessary.

INSTRUCTIONS
Rnd 1: Join White/Pearl thread with sl st over plastic ring. Ch 3, work 17 dc over ring. Join with a sl st to top of beg ch-3. 18 dc.

Rnd 2: Ch 3, dc in same st (st where previous rnd was just joined); *ch 5, sk next 2 dc, work 2 dc in next dc; rep from * 4 more times, ch 5, sk next 2 dc, join with a sl st in top of beg ch-3. Six 2-dc groups with a ch-5 sp between each group.

Rnd 3: Sl st in next dc and then sl st into next sp, ch 1, work (sc, hdc, dc, 2 tr, ch 5, 2 tr, dc, hdc, sc) in same sp (scallop made); *ch 1, sk next 2 dc, work (sc, hdc, dc, 2 tr, ch 5, 2 tr, dc, hdc, sc) in next sp (scallop made); rep from * 4 more times, ch 1, join with a sl st in beg sc. Fasten off.

Rnd 4: With Gold/Gold thread sl st in beg sc, (st where previous rnd was joined), ch 1, sc in same st, sc in each of next 4 sts of first scallop; * † work 2 sc in next sp, then work (ch 5, 2 sc, ch 7, 2 sc, ch 5, 2 sc) in same sp, sc in each of next 5 sts of same scallop †, ch 3, sk next ch-1 sp between scallops, sc in each of next 5 sts of next scallop; rep from * 4 more times, then rep from † to † once, ch 3, sk next ch-1 sp, join with a sl st in beg sc. Fasten off.

FINISHING
Weave in ends. Follow directions for stiffening and blocking snowflakes.

Silver Splendor Snowflake

Easy / Facile / Fácil

FINISHED MEASUREMENTS
Snowflake is approximately 4½" after finishing.

MATERIALS
- Coats & Clark Aunt Lydia's Size 10 Metallic Thread

    10 yd White/Silver

    5 yd Silver/Silver

- ¾" plastic ring
- Hook - 2.00 mm
- Tapestry needle

PATTERN NOTES
See book sections for crocheting over plastic rings and blocking snowflakes if necessary.

SPECIAL STITCHES
Puff St: 3 dc (half closed and joined together) worked in same st.

Picot: Ch 3, sc in 3rd ch from hook.

INSTRUCTIONS
Rnd 1: Join White/Silver thread with sl st over plastic ring. Ch 1, work 24 sc over ring. Join with a sl st to first sc. 24 sc.

Rnd 2: Ch 1, *sc in each of next 2 sc, 2 sc in next sc *, rep from * to * around. Join with a sl st to beg sc. 32 sc.

Rnd 3: Ch 3 (counts as first dc of puff st) *puff st in sc, ch 5, sk next sc *, rep from * to * around. Join with a st st to top of first puff st. 16 puff sts.

Rnd 4: Sl st to first ch-5 sp, (Ch 3, 2 dc, ch 5, 3 dc) in ch-5 sp, sc in next ch-5, *(3 dc, ch 5, 3 dc) in next ch-5 sp, sc in next ch-5 sp *, rep from * to * around. Join with a sl st to beg ch-3. Fasten off White/Silver thread.

Rnd 5: With Silver/Silver thread sl st in any ch-5 lp. Ch 1, * (sc, picot) 4 times in lp, sc in same lp, ch 3, sk next 3 dc, sc in next sc, ch 3, sk next 3 dc *, rep from * to * around. Join with a sl st to beg sc. Fasten off.

FINISHING
Weave in ends. Follow directions for stiffening and blocking snowflakes.

Gold and White Ruffled Snowflake

Easy / Facile / Fácil

FINISHED MEASUREMENTS
Snowflake is approximately 5" after finishing.

MATERIALS
- Coats & Clark Aunt Lydia's Size 10 Metallic Thread

    10 yd White/Pearl

    6 yd Gold/Gold

- ¾" plastic ring
- Hook - 2.00 mm
- Tapestry needle

PATTERN NOTES
See book sections for crocheting over plastic rings and blocking snowflakes if necessary.

SPECIAL STITCHES
Beginning Shell: Ch 3, (2 dc, ch 3, 3 dc) in same sp.

Shell: (3 dc, ch 3, 3 dc) in sp indicated.

Picot: Ch 3, sc in 3rd ch from hook

INSTRUCTIONS
Rnd 1: Join White/Pearl thread with sl st over plastic ring. Work beginning shell over ring, ch 5, (work shell, ch 5) 4 more times. Join with a sl st to top of beg ch-3. 5 shells and 5 ch-5 loops.

Rnd 2: Sl st in next 2 dc and in next ch-3 sp, work beginning shell, ch 4, sc in next loop, ch 4, *work shell in next ch-3 sp, ch 4, sc in next loop, ch 4; rep from * around. Join with a sl st to top of beg ch-3. 5 shells and 10 ch-4 spaces.

Rnd 3: Sl st in next 2 dc and in next ch-3 sp, work beginning shell, ch 5, sc in next ch-4 sp, sc in next sc and in next ch-4 sp, ch 5, *work shell in next ch-3 sp, ch 5, sc in next ch-4 sp, sc in next sc and in next ch-4 sp, ch 5; rep from * around; join with a sl st to top of beg ch-3. Fasten off.

Rnd 4: Join Gold/Gold in first dc of any shell. Ch 8, * † sk next dc, tr in next dc, ch 5, (tr, ch 7, tr) in next ch-3 sp, ch 5, tr in next dc, ch 5, sk next dc, dc in next dc, ch 5, dc in next loop, ch 3, sk next sc, sc in next sc, ch 3, dc in next lp, ch 5, † dc in next dc, ch 5; rep from * 3 times more, then rep from † to † once. Join with a sl st to third ch of beg ch-8. Fasten off.

FINISHING
Weave in ends. Follow directions for stiffening and blocking snowflakes.

Silver and White Picot Star Snowflake

Easy / Facile / Fácil

FINISHED MEASUREMENTS
Snowflake is approximately 5¼" after finishing.

MATERIALS
- Coats & Clark Aunt Lydia's Size 10 Metallic Thread

    9 yd White/Silver

    7 yd Silver/Silver

- 5/8" plastic ring
- Hook - 2.00 mm
- Tapestry needle

PATTERN NOTES
See book sections for crocheting over plastic rings and blocking snowflakes if necessary.

SPECIAL STITCHES
Beginning Cluster (beg cluster): Keeping last lp of each st on hook, work tr in each of next 3 tr (4 lps now on hook), yo hook and draw through all 4 lps on hook.

Cluster: Keeping last lp of each st on hook, work tr in each of next 4 tr (5 lps now on hook), yo hook and draw through all 5 lps on hook.

Picot: Ch 5, sc in 5th ch from hook.

INSTRUCTIONS
Rnd 1: Join White/Silver thread with sl st over plastic ring. Ch 4 (counts as first tr of round), work 3 tr over ring, (ch 3, 4 tr over ring) 5 times, ch 3, join with a sl st in top of beg ch-4. Six 4 tr groups with ch-3 sp between each group.

Rnd 2: Ch 4, work beg cluster over next 3 tr, *ch 6, sc in next sp; ch 6, work cluster over next 4 tr; rep from * 4 times more, ch 6, sc in next sp, ch 6. Join with a sl st in top of beg cluster.

Rnd 3: Sl st into next sp, ch 1, work 6 sc in same sp, work 6 sc in next sp; *ch 10, work 6 sc in each of next 2 sps; rep from * 4 times more, ch 10, join with a sl st in beg sc. Fasten off.

Rnd 4: Join Silver/Silver with a sl st in same sp as you just fastened off. Sl st in next sc (2nd st of first 6 sc group), ch 1, sc in same st and in each of next 3 sc; *† ch 5, sl st in 5th ch from hook (picot made) †; rep from † to † twice more (2 more picots made) sk next sc (last st of this 6-sc group) and sk next sc (first st of next 6-sc group), sc in each of next 4 sc; sk next sc, work 5 sc in next sp; rep from † to † 3 times (3 picots made), work 5 more sc in same sp; sk next sc, sc in each of next 4 sc; rep from * around, ending last rep without working last 4 sc. Join with a sl st in beg sc. Fasten off.

FINISHING
Weave in ends. Follow directions for stiffening and blocking snowflakes.

Silver Sparkle Snowflake

Easy / Facile / Fácil

FINISHED MEASUREMENTS
Snowflake is approximately 5½" after finishing.

MATERIALS
- Coats & Clark Aunt Lydia's Size 10 Metallic Thread

    6 yd White/Silver

    12 yd Silver/Silver

- 5/8" plastic ring
- Hook - 2.00 mm
- Tapestry needle

PATTERN NOTES
See book sections for crocheting over plastic rings and blocking snowflakes if necessary.

SPECIAL STITCHES
Picot: Ch 3, sc in 3rd ch from hook.

Triple picot (tr picot): Picot, ch 7, sl st in 7th ch from hook, picot.

INSTRUCTIONS
Rnd 1: Join White/Silver thread with sl st over plastic ring. Ch 3, work 23 dc over ring. Join with a sl st to top of beg ch-3. 24 dc.

Rnd 2: Ch 1, *sc in next ch sp, ch 4, sk next dc, (tr, ch 3, tr) in next dc, ch 4, sk next dc; rep from * around. Join with a sl st in first sc. 6 sc, 12 tr. Fasten off.

Rnd 3: With Silver/Silver thread sl st in any ch-4 sp. Ch 1, *(sc, hdc, 3 dc) in ch-4 sp, tr in next tr, picot, (3 tr, tr picot, 3 tr) in next ch-3 sp, tr in next tr, picot , (3 dc, hdc, sc) in next ch-4 sp; rep from * around. Join with a sl st to beg sc. Fasten off.

FINISHING
Weave in ends. Follow directions for stiffening and blocking snowflakes.

Conclusion

I hope you enjoyed the patterns. Please consider leaving me a review. I value your opinion and would love to hear from you.

You can also visit my face book fan page to leave a message or comment.

http://www.facebook.com/VickiBeckerAuthor

Visit my author page at Amazon for a list of my other needlework titles!

http://www.amazon.com/author/vickibecker

Visit my web site for more needlework tips and free patterns!

http://vickisdesigns.com

You can email me

vicki@vickisdesigns.com

Books by Vicki Becker

I have needlework books for crochet, knitting, embroidery, coloring, and quilting available at Amazon.com for kindle and in paperback. I have patterns for slippers, afghans, plant hangers, jewelry, household items, and much more! Visit my author page for more information.
http://www.amazon.com/author/vickibecker

 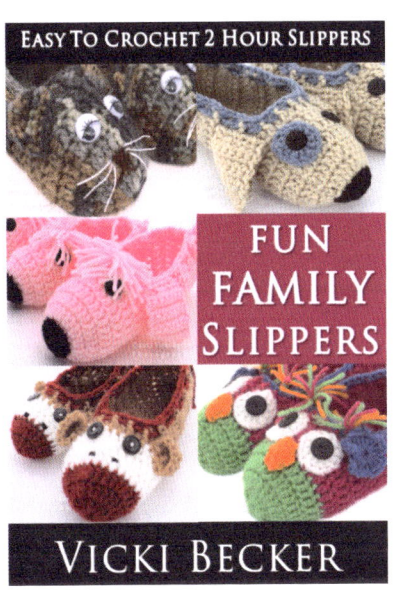 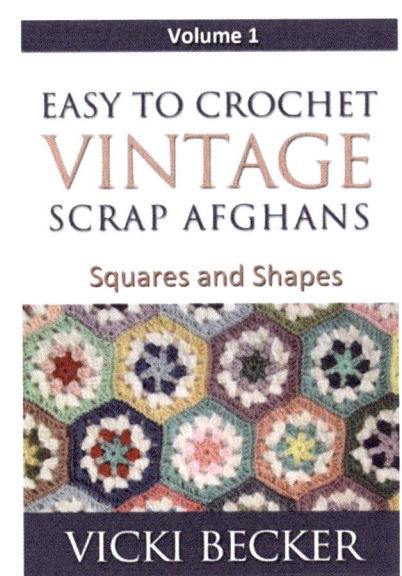

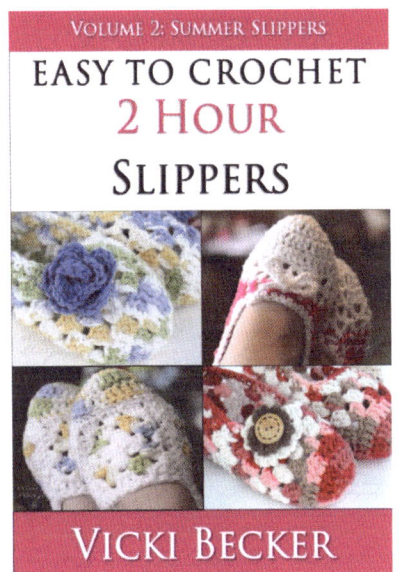 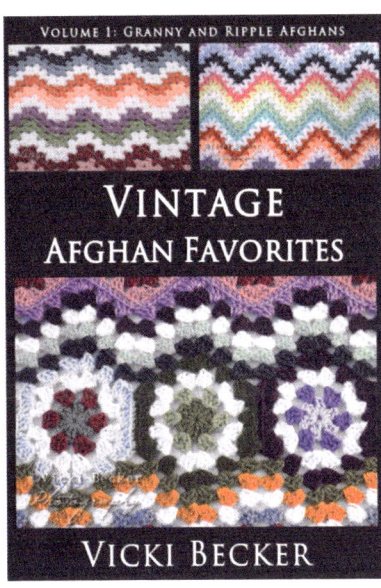 

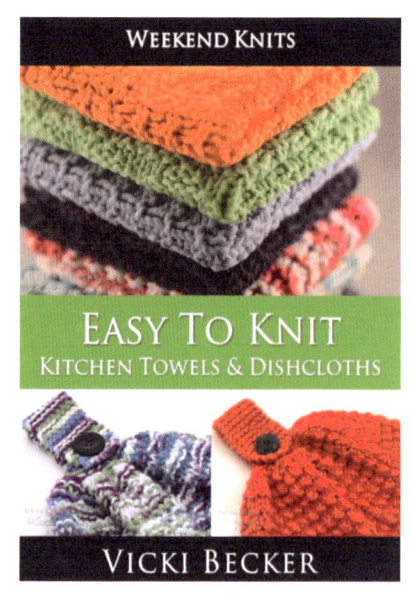
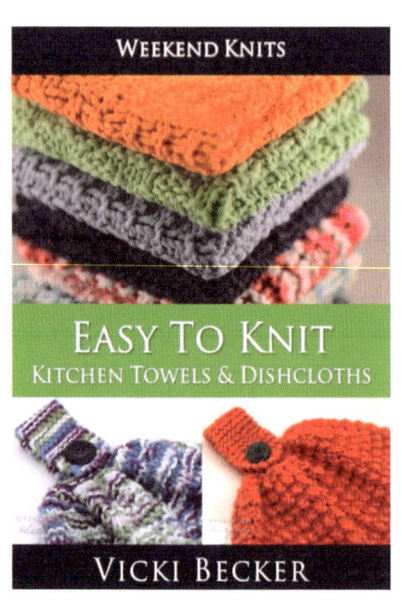
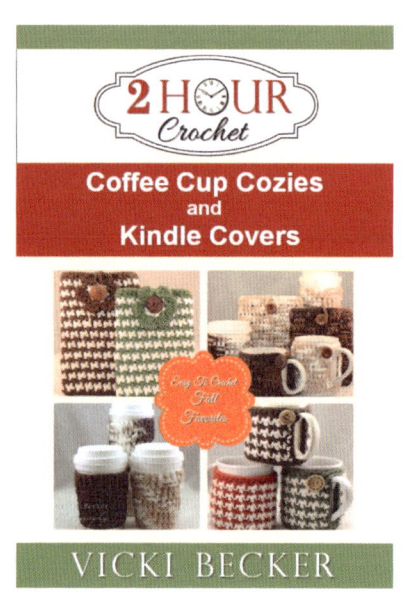
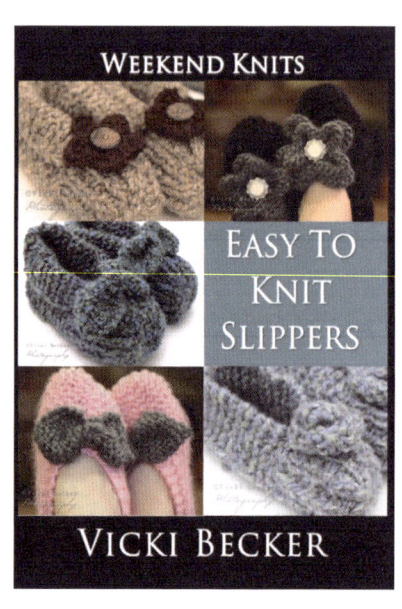

Printed in Dunstable, United Kingdom